GOD IS THE GOSPEL

GOD IS
THE GOSPEL

*Meditations on God's Love
as the Gift of Himself*

STUDY GUIDE DEVELOPED BY DESIRING GOD

CROSSWAY BOOKS
WHEATON, ILLINOIS

God Is the Gospel Study Guide

Copyright © 2008 by Desiring God Foundation

Published by Crossway Books
        a publishing ministry of Good News Publishers
        1300 Crescent Street
        Wheaton, Illinois 60187

This study guide is based on and is a companion to *God Is the Gospel* by John Piper (Crossway Books, 2005).

Cover design: Amy Bristow

Cover photo: iStock

First printing, 2008

Printed in the United States of America

ISBN 978-1-4335-0254-5

BP		16	15	14	13	12	11	10	09	08
14	13	12	11	10	9	8	7	6	5	4	3	2	1

CONTENTS

INTRODUCTION TO THIS STUDY GUIDE

TO BE A CHRISTIAN IS TO embrace the gospel, the good news of Jesus Christ. This good news is the heart of Christianity. But what do we mean by "the gospel"? And why is the gospel "good news"? Too few Christians stop to reflect on these crucial questions.

Those who do seek to answer these questions might say something like this: "Being saved from hell makes the gospel good news. Freedom from a guilty conscience makes the gospel good news. Forgiveness of sins, justification, and eternal life make the gospel good news." And all of these are indeed good gifts of the gospel. Without forgiveness we would be forced to bear our own sins. Without justification we would be forced to provide our own righteousness. Without eternal life we would suffer eternal death. But these blessings simply raise the question again: Why are *these* gospel blessings "good"?

Thankfully, we do not have to speculate on the ultimate good of the gospel. The Bible is clear: the gospel is good news because it brings us to God (1 Peter 3:18). Or, to say it another way, God is the gospel.

If the gospel does not lead us to God as our all-sufficient and everlasting treasure, then, whatever else the gospel may be, it is not good news. Sadly, many people have believed in a truncated version of the gospel that leads them to enjoy God's gifts without being satisfied in the Giver. And if we have embraced the gospel for its many gifts without delighting in God himself in and above all of these gifts, have we genuinely embraced the gospel?

The aim of this study guide is to explore the ultimate good of the good news. The central question that we will seek to answer is this: What do we mean when we say, "God is the gospel"? Our prayer is that this study guide and DVD would be used by God to awaken thousands to the truth that the highest, best, final, and decisive good of the gospel, without which no other gifts would be good, is the glory of God in the face of Christ for our everlasting enjoyment.

This study guide is designed to be used in an eight-session,[1] guided group study that focuses on the *God Is the Gospel* DVD Set.[2] After an introductory lesson, each subsequent lesson examines one thirty-minute session[3] from the *God Is the Gospel* DVD Set. You, the learner, are encouraged to prepare for the viewing of each DVD session by reading and reflecting upon Scripture, by considering key quotations, and by asking yourself penetrating questions. Your preparatory work for each lesson is marked with the heading "Before You Watch the DVD, Study and Prepare" in Lessons 2-7.

The workload is conveniently divided into five daily (and manageable) assignments. There is also a section suggesting further study. This work is to be completed individually before the group convenes to view the DVD and discuss the material.

Throughout this study guide, paragraphs printed in a shaded box (like this one) are excerpts from a book written by John Piper or excerpts taken from the *Desiring God* web site. They are included to supplement the study questions and to summarize key or provocative points.

The second section in Lessons 2-7, entitled "Further Up and Further In," is designed for the learner who wants to explore the concepts and ideas introduced in the lesson in greater detail. This section is not required but will deepen your understanding of the material. This section requires that you read two or three chapters from the book *God Is the Gospel* by John Piper (Wheaton, IL: Crossway Books, 2005) and answer questions drawn from this material. This book is available for free online at www.desiringGod.org in the Online Books section of the Resource Library. You are also welcome to purchase a copy of the book from Desiring God.

The third section in Lessons 2-7, entitled "While You Watch the DVD, Take Notes," is to be completed as the DVD is playing. This section includes fill-in-the-blanks and leaves space for note-taking. You are encouraged to engage with the DVD by filling in the appropriate blanks and writing down other notes that will aid you in the group discussion.

The fourth section in each normal lesson is "After You Watch the DVD, Discuss What You've Learned." Three discussion questions are provided to guide and focus the conversation. You may record, in the spaces provided, notes that will help you contribute to the conversation. Or you may use this space to record things from the discussion that you want to remember.

The fifth and final section is an application section: "After You Discuss, Make Application." You will be challenged to record a "take-away point" and to engage in a certain activity that is a fitting response to the content presented in the lesson.

Group leaders will want to find the Leader's Guide, included at the end of this study guide, immediately.

Life transformation will only occur by the grace of God. Therefore, we highly encourage you to seek the Lord in prayer throughout the learning process. Pray that God would open your eyes to see wonderful things in his Word. Pray that he would grant you the insight and concentration you need in order to get the most from this resource. Pray that God would cause you not merely to understand the truth but also to rejoice in it. And pray that the discussion in your group would be mutually encouraging and edifying. We've included objectives at the beginning of each lesson. These objectives won't be realized without the gracious work of God through prayer.

NOTES

1. While this study guide is ideally suited for an eight-session study, it is possible to complete it in six sessions. The Leader's Guide at the end of this study guide contains a note on one way to complete this study in six weeks. The six-session option may be well-suited for groups that are already familiar with each other or that only have six weeks to complete the study.

2. Although this resource is designed to be used in a group setting, it can also be used by the independent learner. Such learners would have to decide for themselves how to use this resource in the most beneficial way. We would suggest doing everything but the group discussion, if possible.

3. Thirty minutes is only an approximation. Some sessions are longer; others are shorter.

LESSON 1
INTRODUCTION TO *GOD IS THE GOSPEL*

LESSON OBJECTIVES

It is our prayer that after you have finished this lesson . . .

> You will be challenged to reflect upon how you and others in your group view the goodness of the gospel.

> Your curiosity would be roused, and questions would begin to come to mind.

> You will be eager to learn more about how you can learn to keep God central when you celebrate the gospel.

ABOUT YOURSELF

1) What is your name?

2) Tell the group something about yourself that they probably don't already know.

3) Describe your first encounter with the gospel. What was your understanding of the good news?

A PREVIEW OF *GOD IS THE GOSPEL*

1) Summarize the gospel in a short paragraph. What makes the gospel "good news"?

2) The title of this study guide is *God Is the Gospel*. In your own words, explain what you think this sentence might mean. How does this statement relate to your summary of the gospel in Question 1?

LESSON 2
DEFINING "GOD IS THE GOSPEL"
A Companion Study to the God Is the Gospel DVD, Session 1

LESSON OBJECTIVES

It is our prayer that after you have finished this lesson . . .

> You will reflect on what makes heaven so desirable.

> You will glorify God not only for what he does, but also for who he is.

> You will begin to understand how to enjoy created things without committing idolatry.

BEFORE YOU WATCH THE DVD, STUDY AND PREPARE

DAY 1: WHAT'S SO GREAT ABOUT HEAVEN?

The central aim of this course is to explore what makes the "good news" good. One of the ways to begin this exploration is to examine our view of heaven.

QUESTION 1: Following this question, record your thoughts on what heaven will be like. Why will it be enjoyable? How do you think most people in the world picture heaven? How does your understanding differ from the popular conception? Be specific.

The critical question for our generation—and for every generation—is this: If you could have heaven, with no sickness, and with all the friends you ever had on earth, and all the food you ever liked, and all the leisure activities you ever enjoyed, and all the natural beauties that you ever saw, all the physical pleasures you ever tasted, and no human conflict or any natural disasters, could you be satisfied with heaven, if Christ was not there?[1]

Many people in our day profess to believe in God. Indeed, many even claim to believe in Jesus Christ. But it is not always clear *why* people are believing in Jesus.

QUESTION 2: Interact with the following statement: "I've heard that if I believe in Jesus, I won't go to hell, I won't have a guilty conscience, and my marriage and my family life will improve. So for all of these reasons, I think I'll believe in Jesus." Are these good reasons to believe in Jesus? Are they lacking in any way? Explain your answers.

DAY 2: YET I WILL REJOICE IN THE LORD

One of the primary ways to determine what we value the most is to examine how we respond to suffering.

Study the following passage.

HABAKKUK 3:17-18

> [17] *Though the fig tree should not blossom, nor fruit be on the vines, the produce of the olive fail and the fields yield no food, the flock be cut off from the fold and there be no herd in the stalls,* [18] *yet I will rejoice in the LORD; I will take joy in the God of my salvation.*

QUESTION 3: Habakkuk 3:17-18 was written in a time when flocks, herds, and fields were the measure of wealth, success, and livelihood. Rewrite this verse using modern examples of wealth, success, and treasure. Summarize the main point of the passage.

QUESTION 4: Using a modernized version of Habakkuk 3:17-18, how do you think most people would react if verse 17 happened to them? What would this tell you about what they are hoping in?

No one ever said that they learned their deepest lessons of life, or had their sweetest encounters with God, on the sunny days. People go deep with God when the drought comes. That is the way God designed it. Christ aims to be magnified in life most clearly by the way we experience him in our losses. Paul is our example: "We were so utterly burdened beyond our strength that we despaired of life itself. Indeed, we felt that we had received the sentence of death. But that was to make us rely not on ourselves but on God who raises the dead" (2 Corinthians 1:8-9). The design of Paul's suffering was to make radically clear for his own soul, and for ours, that God and God alone is the only treasure who lasts. When everything in life is stripped away except God, and we trust him more because of it, this is gain, and he is glorified.[2]

DAY 3: GOD IS THE GREAT WORKER

Study Isaiah 64:4, 2 Chronicles 16:9, Acts 17:24-25, and Mark 10:45.

ISAIAH 64:4

From of old no one has heard or perceived by the ear, no eye has seen a God besides you, who acts for those who wait for him.

2 CHRONICLES 16:9

For the eyes of the LORD run to and fro throughout the whole earth, to give strong support to those whose heart is blameless toward him.

ACTS 17:24-25

[24] *The God who made the world and everything in it, being Lord of heaven and earth, does not live in temples made by*

man, [25] nor is he served by human hands, as though he needed anything, since he himself gives to all mankind life and breath and everything.

MARK 10:45

For even the Son of Man came not to be served but to serve, and to give his life as a ransom for many.

QUESTION 5: What is the glorious truth that runs throughout all of these passages? Why is this truth "good news?"

What is the greatness of our God? What is His uniqueness in the world? . . . All the other so-called gods try to exalt themselves by making man work for them. In doing so, they only show their weakness. . . . God is unique: "For of old no one has heard or perceived by the ear. . . ." And His uniqueness is that He aims to be the Workman for us, not vice versa. Our job is to "wait for Him."[3]

It is a wonderful thing to know that God works on behalf of his people. But this truth could be subject to a deadly misunderstanding.

QUESTION 6: What is the danger in focusing only on the fact that God works for his people? How could this truth become distorted?

DAY 4: DO WE *ONLY* DESIRE GOD?

The Bible is often explicit in magnifying the all-surpassing value of God. The psalmist proclaims, "I say to the LORD, 'You are my Lord; I have no good apart from you'" (Psalm 16:2). Likewise, Paul says, "But whatever gain I had, I counted as loss for the sake of Christ. Indeed, I count everything as loss because of the surpassing worth of knowing Jesus Christ my Lord" (Philippians 3:7-8).

Study the following passage.

PSALM 73:25-26

> [25] *Whom have I in heaven but you? And there is nothing on earth that I desire besides you.* [26] *My flesh and my heart may fail, but God is the strength of my heart and my portion forever.*

QUESTION 7: Does this passage mean that we should *only* desire God? Is there any place for the enjoyment of other pleasures, whether they be activities or people? Explain your answer.

Our situation as physical creatures is precarious. The question we are asking is not peripheral. It addresses the dangerous condition we are in. We are surrounded by innocent things that are ready to become idols. Innocent sensations are one second away from becoming substitutes for the sweetness of God.[4]

Augustine recognized the danger posed by created things. He wrote, "He loves Thee too little who loves anything together with Thee, which he loves not for Thy sake."[5]

Study the following passage.

1 TIMOTHY 4:4-5

⁴ For everything created by God is good, and nothing is to be rejected if it is received with thanksgiving, ⁵ for it is made holy by the word of God and prayer.

QUESTION 8: Identify three things in your life that you enjoy or delight in. Describe how you can receive and enjoy each of these things in such a way that you do not commit idolatry by loving God too little.

> Enjoying God's gifts without a consciousness of God is no tribute to God himself. Unbelievers do this all the time. Therefore what Paul is teaching us here is that the proper use of physical pleasures in sex and food is that they send our hearts Godward with the joy of gratitude that finds its firmest ground in the goodness of God himself, not in his gifts. This means that if, in the providence of God, these gifts are ever taken away—perhaps by the death of a spouse or the demand for a feeding tube—the deepest joy that we had through them will not be taken away, because God is still good (see Hab. 3:17-18).[6]

DAY 5: FEASTING AND FASTING

The world is full of wonderful gifts from God. The creation of the material world, including our bodies with all five senses, was

God's idea. But why did he make the world in this way? Are created things merely a temptation to idolatry?

Study Psalm 19:1, Psalm 63:1, and John 6:35.

PSALM 19:1

The heavens declare the glory of God, and the sky above proclaims his handiwork.

PSALM 63:1

O God, you are my God; earnestly I seek you; my soul thirsts for you; my flesh faints for you, as in a dry and weary land where there is no water.

JOHN 6:35

Jesus said to them, "I am the bread of life; whoever comes to me shall not hunger, and whoever believes in me shall never thirst."

QUESTION 9: From these passages, why do you think God created so many wonderful things (like the stars and bread and water)? What is the purpose of created things?

Why did God create bread and design human beings to need it for life? He could have created life that has no need of food. He is God. He could have done it any way he pleased. Why bread? And why hunger and thirst? My answer is very simple: He created bread so that we would have some idea of what the Son of God is like when he says, "I am the bread of life" (John 6:35). And he created the rhythm of thirst and satisfaction so that we would have some idea of what faith in Christ is like when Jesus said, "He who believes in me shall never thirst" (John 6:35).[7]

So it is possible to glorify God through feasting, if we see that the physical bread is a representation of the Bread of Life. But feasting is not the only way that we glorify God through created things.

Study the following passage.

MATTHEW 9:14-17

[14] *Then the disciples of John came to him, saying, "Why do we and the Pharisees fast, but your disciples do not fast?"* [15] *And Jesus said to them, "Can the wedding guests mourn as long as the bridegroom is with them? The days will come when the bridegroom is taken away from them, and then they will fast.* [16] *No one puts a piece of unshrunk cloth on an old garment, for the patch tears away from the garment, and a worse tear is made.* [17] *Neither is new wine put into old wineskins. If it is, the skins burst and the wine is spilled and the skins are destroyed. But new wine is put into fresh wineskins, and so both are preserved."*

QUESTION 10: According to this passage, when will the disciples of Jesus fast? Why will they fast? In light of this, how does fasting glorify God?

FURTHER UP AND FURTHER IN

Note: The "Further Up and Further In" section is for those who want to study more. It is a section for further reference and going deeper. The phrase "further up and further in" is borrowed from C. S. Lewis.

As noted in the introduction, each lesson in this study guide provides the opportunity for you to do further study. In this section, you will have the opportunity to read two or three chapters of *God Is the Gospel* and answer some questions about what you read.

Read the Introduction to *God Is the Gospel* (pages 11-17).

In the Introduction, John Piper repeatedly emphasizes the need for Christians to see God as the greatest gift in the gospel. He says, "And not one gospel blessing will be enjoyed by anyone for whom the gospel's greatest gift was not the Lord himself."[8] Again he writes, "Can we really say that our people are being prepared for heaven where Christ himself, not his gifts, will be the supreme pleasure? And if our people are unfit for that, will they even go there? Is not the faith that takes us to heaven the foretaste of the feast of Christ?"[9]

QUESTION 11: If we don't see God as the highest and best gift of the gospel, should we question whether we have genuinely been saved? Explain your answer.

Read Chapter 1, "The Gospel—Proclamation and Explanation," in *God Is the Gospel* (pages 19-23).

QUESTION 12: What are the two aspects of the gospel that John Piper discusses in this chapter? What is the difference between them? Why is it important to preserve both of them?

Read Chapter 2, "The Gospel—The Biblical Scope of Its Meaning," in *God Is the Gospel* (pages 25-38).

QUESTION 13: What is included in "the gospel" when we are viewing the gospel as an event? Be specific, and cite Scripture in your answer.

QUESTION 14: What is included in "the gospel" when we are viewing the gospel in terms of its accomplishments? Be specific, and cite Scripture in your answer. Are these accomplishments only the *effects* of the gospel or are they part of the gospel itself?

QUESTION 15: At the end of this chapter, John Piper compares the gospel to a diamond. Why is it crucial to enjoy the diamond as a whole and not merely the various facets of the diamond? What happens if you only embrace some of the facets of the gospel but not the ultimate good of the gospel?

WHILE YOU WATCH THE DVD, TAKE NOTES

God is the gospel means that God is the _____, _____, _____, and _____ good in the _____ _____.

What simple observation did John Piper's granddaughter Millie make?

What biblical text sustained John Piper in his early ministry?

What is the purpose of created things?

According to John Piper, what is the meaning of fasting?

AFTER YOU WATCH THE DVD, DISCUSS WHAT YOU'VE LEARNED

1) Discuss whether or not you would want to go to a perfect heaven if Jesus were not there. Why is this such a crucial question to ask?

2) What is the difference between rejoicing in God for who he is and rejoicing in God for what he does? Why is it dangerous to only emphasize the latter without mentioning the former?

3) How should we reconcile biblical statements like "On earth there is nothing I desire besides you" with the reality that all of us enjoy created things in some mea-

sure? What implications does this have for our daily lives?

AFTER YOU DISCUSS, MAKE APPLICATION

1) What was the most meaningful part of this lesson for you? Was there a sentence, concept, or idea that really struck you? Why? Record your thoughts in the space below.

2) Make a list of five legitimate pleasures in your life. Spend time planning how you can glorify God this week through these pleasures by enjoying them and by refraining from them. After enacting your plan, reflect on this experience in the space below.

NOTES

1. Excerpt taken from *God Is the Gospel*, page 15.

2. Excerpt taken from *Don't Waste Your Life*, page 73.

3. Excerpt taken from *Desiring God*, pages 169-170.

4. Excerpt taken from *When I Don't Desire God*, page 178.

5. As quoted in *Desiring God*, page 166.

6. Excerpt taken from *When I Don't Desire God*, page 187.

7. Excerpt taken from *God Is the Gospel*, page 140.

8. Excerpt taken from *God Is the Gospel*, page 12.

9. Excerpt taken from *God Is the Gospel*, pages 15-16.

LESSON 3
GOD IS THE GOSPEL IN WONDERS AND IN PRAYER
A Companion Study to the God Is the Gospel DVD, Session 2

LESSON OBJECTIVES

It is our prayer that after you have finished this lesson . . .

> ❯ You will earnestly desire spiritual gifts in a way that keeps God central.
> ❯ You will seek to pray in such a way that you are not using God for your own ends.
> ❯ You will embrace the truth that God has given prayer to us for the sake of his mission in the world.

BEFORE YOU WATCH THE DVD, STUDY AND PREPARE

DAY 1: MANIFESTATIONS OF THE SPIRIT

Though it is a controversial subject, John Piper and Desiring God wholeheartedly embrace the biblical teaching on the continuing work of the Spirit in giving charismatic gifts to the church.[1] The biblical passage that most clearly addresses the charismatic work of the Spirit is 1 Corinthians 12-14.

Study the following passage.

1 CORINTHIANS 12:4-12

[4] Now there are varieties of gifts, but the same Spirit; [5] and there are varieties of service, but the same Lord; [6] and there are varieties of activities, but it is the same God who empowers them all in everyone. [7] To each is given the manifestation of the Spirit for the common good. [8] For to one is given through the Spirit the utterance of wisdom, and to another the utterance of knowledge according to the same Spirit, [9] to another faith by the same Spirit, to another gifts of healing by the one Spirit, [10] to another the working of miracles, to another prophecy, to another the ability to distinguish between spirits, to another various kinds of tongues, to another the interpretation of tongues. [11] All these are empowered by one and the same Spirit, who apportions to each one individually as he wills. [12] For just as the body is one and has many members, and all the members of the body, though many, are one body, so it is with Christ.

QUESTION 1: Summarize the main point of this passage. According to this text, why does God supply manifestations of the Spirit?

As we noted above, the clearest teaching on spiritual gifts is found in 1 Corinthians 12 and 1 Corinthians 14. We believe it is highly significant that 1 Corinthians 13, the chapter on the nature of Christian love, comes between these two chapters on the manifestations of the Spirit.

Study 1 Corinthians 12:27-31 and 1 Corinthians 14:1.

1 CORINTHIANS 12:27-31

[27] *Now you are the body of Christ and individually members of it.* [28] *And God has appointed in the church first apostles, second prophets, third teachers, then miracles, then gifts of healing, helping, administrating, and various kinds of tongues.* [29] *Are all apostles? Are all prophets? Are all teachers? Do all work miracles?* [30] *Do all possess gifts of healing? Do all speak with tongues? Do all interpret?* [31] *But earnestly desire the higher gifts. And I will show you a still more excellent way.*

1 CORINTHIANS 14:1

Pursue love, and earnestly desire the spiritual gifts, especially that you may prophesy.

QUESTION 2: What is the "more excellent way" mentioned in 1 Corinthians 12:31? Should believers today seek to obey the commands in 1 Corinthians 12:31 and 14:1? What are some of the dangers in seeking the powerful manifestations of the Spirit?

DAY 2: THE FAITH OF SIMON THE MAGICIAN
Study the following passage.

ACTS 8:9-24

[9] *But there was a man named Simon, who had previously practiced magic in the city and amazed the people of Samaria, saying*

that he himself was somebody great. [10] They all paid attention to him, from the least to the greatest, saying, "This man is the power of God that is called Great." [11] And they paid attention to him because for a long time he had amazed them with his magic. [12] But when they believed Philip as he preached good news about the kingdom of God and the name of Jesus Christ, they were baptized, both men and women. [13] Even Simon himself believed, and after being baptized he continued with Philip. And seeing signs and great miracles performed, he was amazed. [14] Now when the apostles at Jerusalem heard that Samaria had received the word of God, they sent to them Peter and John, [15] who came down and prayed for them that they might receive the Holy Spirit, [16] for he had not yet fallen on any of them, but they had only been baptized in the name of the Lord Jesus. [17] Then they laid their hands on them and they received the Holy Spirit. [18] Now when Simon saw that the Spirit was given through the laying on of the apostles' hands, he offered them money, [19] saying, "Give me this power also, so that anyone on whom I lay my hands may receive the Holy Spirit." [20] But Peter said to him, "May your silver perish with you, because you thought you could obtain the gift of God with money! [21] You have neither part nor lot in this matter, for your heart is not right before God. [22] Repent, therefore, of this wickedness of yours, and pray to the Lord that, if possible, the intent of your heart may be forgiven you. [23] For I see that you are in the gall of bitterness and in the bond of iniquity." [24] And Simon answered, "Pray for me to the Lord, that nothing of what you have said may come upon me."

QUESTION 3: What is the central sin of Simon the magician throughout this passage? Underline every place that reveals this sin. How is this sin still present in the world today?

QUESTION 4: According to Acts 8:13, Simon "believed" and was "baptized." Do you believe that Simon was genuinely born again at this point? Why or why not? Is desire for spiritual power good evidence that someone has been born again?

> It is not only the material world that tempts us to love the gift above the giver. The spiritual world has the same dangers. Love for signs and wonders may displace love for God just like any material thing.
>
> This should caution us about a misplaced emphasis on miracles in leading people to Christ. . . . Like all God's gifts, signs and wonders witness to the nature and character of God, especially his grace. But, as with material gifts, miraculous gifts may lure our hearts to themselves and not to God. This is why we must keep emphasizing that God is the gospel.[2]

DAY 3: SIGNS AND WONDERS

The Bible is full of examples of God authenticating his work and his messengers by the use of signs and wonders. Jesus was "a man attested . . . by God with mighty works and wonders and signs that God did through him in your midst" (Acts 2:22). "Stephen, full of grace and power, was doing great wonders and signs among the people" (Acts 6:8). The apostle Paul said, "For I will not venture to speak of anything except what Christ has accomplished through me to bring the Gentiles to obedience—by word and deed, by the power of signs and wonders, by the power of the Spirit of God" (Romans 15:18-19). The book of Hebrews tells us that God bore witness to the message of salvation "by signs and wonders and various miracles and by gifts of the Holy Spirit distributed according to his will" (Hebrews 2:4). But are signs and wonders always a reliable indicator that God is at work?

Study Matthew 24:23-24 and 2 Thessalonians 2:9-10.

MATTHEW 24:23-24

[23] *"Then if anyone says to you, 'Look, here is the Christ!' or 'There he is!' do not believe it.* [24] *For false christs and false prophets will arise and perform great signs and wonders, so as to lead astray, if possible, even the elect."*

2 THESSALONIANS 2:9-10

[9] *The coming of the lawless one is by the activity of Satan with all power and false signs and wonders,* [10] *and with all wicked deception for those who are perishing, because they refused to love the truth and so be saved.*

QUESTION 5: In light of these texts, are signs and wonders sure indicators of a true work of God? Why or why not? How can we differentiate between a true work of God and the work of demonic forces?

Study the following passage.

JOHN 7:1-5

> *¹ After this Jesus went about in Galilee. He would not go about in Judea, because the Jews were seeking to kill him. ² Now the Jews' Feast of Booths was at hand. ³ So his brothers said to him, "Leave here and go to Judea, that your disciples also may see the works you are doing. ⁴ For no one works in secret if he seeks to be known openly. If you do these things, show yourself to the world." ⁵ For not even his brothers believed in him.*

QUESTION 6: Looking only at 7:3-4, do Jesus' brothers appear to be genuine in their desire for Jesus to display his works to the world? How does verse 5 undercut the genuineness of their motives? What does this passage teach us about the desire to see power displayed?

DAY 4: BETRAYING GOD WITH PRAYER

How we pray reveals the desires of our hearts. That is why J. I. Packer has said, "I believe that prayer is the measure of the man, spiritually, in a way that nothing else is, so that how we pray is as important a question as we can ever face."[3]

Study the following passage.

JAMES 4:2-5

> *² You desire and do not have, so you murder. You covet and cannot obtain, so you fight and quarrel. You do not have, because*

you do not ask. ³ You ask and do not receive, because you ask wrongly, to spend it on your passions. ⁴ You adulterous people! Do you not know that friendship with the world is enmity with God? Therefore whoever wishes to be a friend of the world makes himself an enemy of God. ⁵ Or do you suppose it is to no purpose that the Scripture says, "He yearns jealously over the spirit that he has made to dwell in us"?

QUESTION 7: Give two reasons why the people addressed in the passage above did not have what they wanted.

QUESTION 8: What is the significance of the fact that James calls these believers "adulterous people" (literally, "adulteresses")? How does asking with wrong motives turn prayer into adultery?

DAY 5: WHEN PRAYER MALFUNCTIONS

Prayer exists for the glory of God. Jesus said, "Whatever you ask in my name, this I will do, that the Father may be glorified in the Son" (John 14:13). Prayer also exists for the sake of our joy. Again, Jesus said, "Ask, and you will receive, that your joy may be full" (John 16:24). These two goals of prayer are not at odds. God is most glorified in you when you are most satisfied in him.

QUESTION 9: In light of the fact that prayer exists for the glory of God, is it wrong to pray for healing, for a new job, for family, or for similar things? Why or why not? Is it possible to pray for these things in such a way that God is displeased with these prayers? Explain your answer.

If we do not watch carefully over our souls, prayer can easily malfunction. Read the following quotation by John Piper.

Probably the number one reason prayer malfunctions in the hands of believers is that we try to turn a wartime walkie-talkie into a domestic intercom. Until you know that life is war, you cannot know what prayer is for. Prayer is for the accomplishment of a wartime mission. It is as though the field commander (Jesus) called in the troops, gave them a crucial mission (go and bear fruit), handed each of them a personal transmitter coded to the frequency of the General's headquarters, and said, "Comrades, the General has a mission for you. He aims to see it accomplished. And to that end he has authorized me to give each of you personal access to him through these transmitters. If you stay true to his mission and seek his victory first, he will always be as close as your transmitter, to give tactical advice and to send air cover when you need it."

But what have millions of Christians done? We have stopped believing that we are in a war. No urgency, no watching, no vigilance. No strategic planning. Just easy peace and prosperity. And what did we do with the walkie-talkie? We tried to rig it up as an intercom in our houses and cabins and boats and cars—not to call in firepower for conflict with a mortal enemy but to ask for more comforts in the den.[4]

QUESTION 10: What is the chief way that prayer malfunctions in the hands of believers? Have you ever been guilty of misusing prayer? If life is war, what are we fighting for?

FURTHER UP AND FURTHER IN

Read Chapter 3, "The Gospel—'Behold Your God!'" in *God Is the Gospel* (pages 41-56).

QUESTION 11: Interact with the following statement from John Piper in this chapter: "Christ did not die to forgive sinners who go on treasuring anything above seeing and savoring God. And people who would be happy in heaven if Christ were not there, will not be there. The gospel is not a way to get people to heaven; it is a way to get people to God. It's a way of overcoming every obstacle to everlasting joy in God. If we don't want God above all things, we have not been converted by the gospel."[5]

QUESTION 12: On pages 52-53, John Piper lists a number of "diverse excellencies" that make Christ admirable. Choose two or three of these excellencies and reflect upon them. Why does the diversity of the excellencies make Christ more valuable than he would be otherwise?

QUESTION 13: Much of this chapter emphasizes the need to *see* the glory of Christ. Should we understand this "seeing" to be physical sight? Should we expect our sight of Christ's glory to be constant and unchanging? How do you know? Cite Scripture in your answer.

Read Chapter 4, "The Gospel—The Glory of Christ, the Image of God," in *God Is the Gospel* (pages 59-74).

QUESTION 14: On page 64, John Piper quotes Jonathan Edwards on two distinct types of knowledge. What are these two types of knowledge? What is the difference between them? What analogy does Edwards provide to illustrate the difference?

QUESTION 15: This chapter emphasizes the sovereign, creative power of God in causing gospel light to shine in our darkened hearts. What misunderstanding does John Piper guard against on pages 68-69? What two truths must we hold together, even if they seem to be in tension?

WHILE YOU WATCH THE DVD, TAKE NOTES

Wanting _____ from God for _____ _____ is no sign of being _____ ___ _____.

What lesson did John Piper learn from Deuteronomy 13:1-3?

_____ Jesus does not _____ you if you're _____ him to do the _____ _____.

What analogy does John Piper use to illustrate James 4:2-5?

Does John Piper believe that it is wrong to pray for healing, or for the kids to turn out well, or for a new job?

AFTER YOU WATCH THE DVD, DISCUSS WHAT YOU'VE LEARNED

1) Discuss how we can test ourselves to know whether we are seeking God's power for the right reasons.

2) How do we avoid turning God into a cuckold with prayer?

3) Give examples of ways that people turn the wartime walkie-talkie into a domestic intercom. Be specific.

AFTER YOU DISCUSS, MAKE APPLICATION

1) What was the most meaningful part of this lesson for you? Was there a sentence, concept, or idea that really struck you? Why? Record your thoughts in the space below.

2) Spend at least ten minutes this week reflecting on your prayer life. Make a list of your most common prayer requests and petitions. What does your prayer life reveal about the desires of your heart? If necessary, spend time repenting of any desires that have turned God into a cuckold. Record your reflections below.

NOTES

1. For further study on the charismatic gifts, see the Spiritual Gifts section in the Topic Index of the Resource Library at the Desiring God web site.
2. Excerpt taken from *God Is the Gospel*, page 142.
3. As quoted in *When I Don't Desire God*, page 139.
4. Excerpt taken from *Let the Nations Be Glad*, page 49.
5. Excerpt taken from *God Is the Gospel*, page 47.

LESSON 4
THE LOVE OF GOD WHEN GOD IS THE GOSPEL
A Companion Study to the God Is the Gospel DVD, Session 3

LESSON OBJECTIVES

It is our prayer that after you have finished this lesson . . .

> You will understand how you can honor God in life and death.

> You will see the connection between the greatness of God's love and the greatness of God himself.

> You will embrace a biblical view of the love of God.

BEFORE YOU WATCH THE DVD, STUDY AND PREPARE

DAY 1: CHRISTIAN HEDONISM

The theology that is articulated in this study is often called Christian Hedonism. Christian Hedonism means that God's passion to be glorified and our passion to be satisfied are not two passions; they are one. God is most glorified in us when we are most satisfied in him. In this section we will seek to provide a clear biblical basis for Christian Hedonism.

Study the following passage.

PHILIPPIANS 1:19-21

> [19] *For I know that through your prayers and the help of the Spirit of Jesus Christ this will turn out for my deliverance,* [20] *as it is my eager expectation and hope that I will not be at all ashamed, but that with full courage now as always Christ will be honored in my body, whether by life or by death.* [21] *For to me to live is Christ, and to die is gain.*

QUESTION 1: According to this passage, what is the opposite of being ashamed? Why is this significant?

The opposite of being shamed is being honored. Yes, usually. But Paul was a very unusual person. And Christians ought to be very unusual people. For Paul, the opposite of being shamed was not *his* being honored, but *Christ's* being honored through him. "It is my eager expectation and hope that I will not be at all ashamed, but that . . . Christ will be honored in my body."

What you love determines what you feel shame about. If you love for men to make much of you, you will feel shame when they don't. But if you love for men to make much of Christ, then you will feel shame if he is belittled on your account. . . .

> Whenever something is of tremendous value to you, and you cherish its beauty or power or uniqueness, you want to draw others' attention to it and waken in them the same joy. That is why Paul's all-consuming goal in life was for Christ to be magnified. Christ was of infinite value to Paul, and so Paul longed for others to see and savor this value. That is what it means to magnify Christ—to show the magnitude of his value.[1]

QUESTION 2: How do you honor Christ "by life"? How do you honor him "by death"?

DAY 2: DEATH IS GAIN!

Look again at Philippians 1.

PHILIPPIANS 1:19-23

> [19] *For I know that through your prayers and the help of the Spirit of Jesus Christ this will turn out for my deliverance,* [20] *as it is my eager expectation and hope that I will not be at all ashamed, but that with full courage now as always Christ will be honored in my body, whether by life or by death.* [21] *For to me to live is Christ, and to die is gain.* [22] *If I am to live in the flesh, that means fruitful labor for me. Yet which I shall choose I cannot tell.* [23] *I am hard pressed between the two. My desire is to depart and be with Christ, for that is far better.*

QUESTION 3: Reflect on the statement "To die is gain" in verse 21. How do you understand this phrase? How does it relate to the surrounding context? Record your reflections below.

> But how are we to magnify Christ in death? Or to put it another way: How can we die so that in our dying the surpassing value of Christ, the magnitude of his worth, becomes visible? Paul's answer here in Philippians 1 is found first in the connection between verse 20 and verse 21. These verses are connected by the word "for" or "because." Boil it down to the words about death: "My eager expectation is that Christ be honored in my body by death, for to me to die is gain." In other words, if you experience death as gain, you magnify Christ in death.[2]

QUESTION 4: How does Philippians 1:19-23 support the statement, "God is most glorified in us when we are most satisfied in him"?

DAY 3: GOD'S SALVATION AND GOD HIMSELF

Study the following passage.

PHILIPPIANS 3:7-8

> [7] *But whatever gain I had, I counted as loss for the sake of Christ.* [8] *Indeed, I count everything as loss because of the surpassing worth of knowing Christ Jesus my Lord. For his sake I have suffered the loss of all things and count them as rubbish, in order that I may gain Christ.*

QUESTION 5: How does this passage display the glory of Christ? How does this passage relate to Philippians 1:19-23 (which you studied earlier in this lesson)?

Study Psalm 63:3 and Psalm 70:4.

PSALM 63:3

> *Because your steadfast love is better than life, my lips will praise you.*

PSALM 70:4

> *May all who seek you rejoice and be glad in you! May those who love your salvation say evermore, "God is great!"*

QUESTION 6: In these passages, what is the relationship between the love of God and the salvation of God on the one hand

and God himself on the other? How do these texts reinforce the truth that God is the gospel?

DAY 4: WHAT IS LOVE?

Love is one of the most common words in the English language. We love our families. We love TV shows. We love sports. We love food. The world rings with the sounds of love. But what do we mean by *love*?

QUESTION 7: Attempt to provide a secular definition of love. Now provide your own definition of love. Note any significant differences between the secular definition and your definition.

One of the central assumptions of Christian Hedonism is that God is unswervingly committed to his own glory. The Bible is clear on this point. Listen to these words from the book of Isaiah.

ISAIAH 43:6-7

> [6] *I will say to the north, Give up, and to the south, Do not withhold; bring my sons from afar and my daughters from the end of the earth,* [7] *everyone who is called by my name, whom I created for my glory, whom I formed and made.*

ISAIAH 43:25

I, I am he who blots out your transgressions for my own sake, and I will not remember your sins.

ISAIAH 48:9-11

[9] *For my name's sake I defer my anger, for the sake of my praise I restrain it for you, that I may not cut you off.* [10] *Behold, I have refined you, but not as silver; I have tried you in the furnace of affliction.* [11] *For my own sake, for my own sake, I do it, for how should my name be profaned? My glory I will not give to another.*

QUESTION 8: What is the relationship between God's passion for his glory and God's love for sinners? If God always acts for the sake of his name, where does that leave his love for us?

DAY 5: THE SHOCKING LOVE OF JESUS

In this final section, we will seek to understand the relationship between God's passion for his glory and God's love for sinners.

Study the following passage.

JOHN 11:1-6

[1] *Now a certain man was ill, Lazarus of Bethany, the village of Mary and her sister Martha.* [2] *It was Mary who anointed the Lord with ointment and wiped his feet with her hair, whose brother Lazarus was ill.* [3] *So the sisters sent to him, saying,*

"Lord, he whom you love is ill." ⁴ But when Jesus heard it he said, "This illness does not lead to death. It is for the glory of God, so that the Son of God may be glorified through it." ⁵ Now Jesus loved Martha and her sister and Lazarus. ⁶ So, when he heard that Lazarus was ill, he stayed two days longer in the place where he was.

QUESTION 9: Underline every reference to the love of Jesus. Circle every reference to the glory of God.

QUESTION 10: Explain the logic between verse 5 and verse 6. In particular, focus on the use of the word "So" in verse 6. (Note: Some English translations mistranslate this word as "Yet." We consider this to be a serious mistake. The Greek word *oun* at the beginning of verse 6 means "so" or "therefore.")

The first astonishing thing in this text is that Jesus did not depart right away so as to get there in time to heal Lazarus. "He stayed two days longer in the place where he was" (v. 6). In other words, he intentionally delayed and let Lazarus die. The second astonishing thing here is that this delay is described as the result of Jesus' love for his friends. Notice the word "so" at the beginning of verse 6: "Jesus loved Martha and her sister and Lazarus. *So* . . . he stayed two days longer." Jesus let Lazarus die *because* he loved him and his sisters.[3]

FURTHER UP AND FURTHER IN

Read Chapter 5, "The Gospel—Confirmed by Its Glory, the Internal Testimony of the Holy Spirit," in *God Is the Gospel* (pages 77-85).

QUESTION 11: How does John Piper define the internal testimony of the Holy Spirit? How does this testimony differ from a voice in someone's head saying, "This book is true"?

God testifies to us of his reality and the reality of his Son and of the gospel by giving us life from the dead, so that we come alive to his self-authenticating glory in the gospel. In that instant we do not reason from premises to conclusions; rather we see that we are awake, and there is not even a prior human judgment about it to lean on. When Lazarus wakened in the tomb by the call or the "testimony" of Christ, he knew without reasoning that he was alive and that this call awakened him.[4]

QUESTION 12: On pages 82-83, John Piper discusses two aspects of the ground of our faith. What are these two aspects, and why are they important? How do these two convictions help settle the question of how uneducated people can possess unshakable faith?

Read Chapter 6, "The Gospel—The Glory of Christ in Evangelism, Missions, and Sanctification," in *God Is the Gospel* (pages 87-97).

QUESTION 13: In relation to missions and evangelism, why is it so crucial "to understand that saving faith is grounded on a spiritual sight of the glory of God in the gospel"?[5]

Few minds have surpassed the mind of Jonathan Edwards in greatness of mental vigor and creativity and insight and comprehensiveness. But Edwards had a huge burden for ordinary people in New England, and for Indians on the frontier, and for "Mahometans" across the seas. He points out that these people simply will not be able to come to real, well-grounded faith in the gospel . . . if they cannot come by a spiritual perception of the self-authenticating glory of God in it. . . .

And even if people can come to a sense of strong probability that the gospel is true on the basis of historical reasonings, this will not suffice for sustaining a person in suffering and torture.[6]

QUESTION 14: On pages 90-94, John Piper discusses 2 Corinthians 3:18: "And we all, with unveiled face, beholding the glory of the Lord, are being transformed into the same image from one degree of glory to another. For this comes from the Lord who is the Spirit." What three observations does he draw from this text? What effect should these observations have on our doctrine of sanctification?

QUESTION 15: How does our progressive sanctification in this life relate to our final glorification on the last day? Cite Scripture in your answer.

WHILE YOU WATCH THE DVD, TAKE NOTES

How do we magnify Christ as we breathe our last breath?

Fill in the blank with what we might expect Psalm 70:4 to say: Let all those who love your salvation say evermore, "Great is

_____ _____."

According to John Piper, what does the world mean by love?

According to John Piper, what is the biblical definition of love?

God is the _____ _____ in the universe for whom _____ is the _____ way to _____.

AFTER YOU WATCH THE DVD, DISCUSS WHAT YOU'VE LEARNED

1) Discuss Paul's provocative statement that "Death is gain." How can this statement revolutionize your life?

2) Why is God not a megalomaniac if he always seeks to exalt himself in everything he does?

3) Discuss the difference between the world's definition of love and the biblical definition of love as expressed in John 11. Why is biblical love so shocking?

AFTER YOU DISCUSS, MAKE APPLICATION

1) What was the most meaningful part of this lesson for you? Was there a sentence, concept, or idea that really struck you? Why? Record your thoughts in the space below.

2) Meditate on the story of Lazarus from John 11. Lazarus' death, as tragic as it was, was an expression of Jesus' love. Are there any difficult circumstances or instances of suffering and affliction in your life that are seen in a new light after reflecting on this story? Record your reflections below.

NOTES

1. Excerpt taken from *Don't Waste Your Life*, page 65.
2. Excerpt taken from *Don't Waste Your Life*, page 67.
3. Excerpt taken from *God Is the Gospel*, pages 152-153.
4. Excerpt taken from *God Is the Gospel*, page 80.
5. Excerpt taken from *God Is the Gospel*, page 89.
6. Excerpt taken from *God Is the Gospel*, pages 87-88.

LESSON 5
DELIGHTING IN GOD DELIGHTING IN US
A Companion Study to the God Is the Gospel DVD, Session 4

LESSON OBJECTIVES

It is our prayer that after you have finished this lesson . . .

> ⟩ You will be able to discern the difference between God-honoring gratitude and idolatrous gratitude.

> ⟩ You will understand the relationship between God's delight in himself and his delight in his people.

> ⟩ You will be able to respond to the objection that God is a needy egomaniac because he demands that we worship him.

BEFORE YOU WATCH THE DVD, STUDY AND PREPARE

DAY 1: THE GREAT SIN OF INGRATITUDE

Study the following passage.

ROMANS 1:18-23

[18] For the wrath of God is revealed from heaven against all ungodliness and unrighteousness of men, who by their unrighteousness suppress the truth. [19] For what can be known about God is plain to them, because God has shown it to them. [20] For his invisible attributes, namely, his eternal power and divine nature, have been clearly perceived, ever since the creation of the world, in the things that have been made. So they are without excuse. [21] For although they knew God, they did not honor him as God or give thanks to him, but they became futile in their thinking, and their foolish hearts were darkened. [22] Claiming to be wise, they became fools, [23] and exchanged the glory of the immortal God for images resembling mortal man and birds and animals and creeping things.

QUESTION 1: Underline every reference to human sin in this passage. What two great sins are described in verse 21? How do these sins manifest themselves?

From sea to shining sea the creation shouts that *God* has eternal power, *God* is the infinitely marvelous Being, *God* is the Maker of all that is, and we are utterly dependent on his absolutely free choices to create and sustain our life or not, and we should therefore glorify *him* and not ourselves and give thanks to *him* and not take credit for ourselves. *But proud people don't say thanks.* Gratitude is the echo of grace reverberating through the hollows of the human heart. But proud people don't need grace. They don't think their hearts are hollow without God. They are filled with wisdom! So "claiming to be wise, they exchange the glory of the immortal God for images." Proud people don't say thanks. Tight-lipped, they take the diamond of God's glory, enter the pawn shop of pride, and hock it for the broken marble of self-reliance. Then they take this little idol home, set it on the mantel of their mind, and bow down to it in a hundred different ways every day. "Although we knew God, we did not glorify him as God or give thanks to him but became futile in our thinking . . . claiming to be wise." Proud people don't say thanks.[1]

It's clear from Romans 1:21 that one of the central transgressions of all human beings is ingratitude. But does the fact that ingratitude is always wrong mean that gratitude is always right?

QUESTION 2: Is it possible to be thankful for the wrong reasons? In other words, could a person genuinely thank God in such a way that his or her gratitude was itself a sin? Be specific in your answer.

DAY 2: IDOLATROUS GRATITUDE

All Christians love the cross of Christ. It is the only hope that we have for salvation. Thus, Christians are rightfully grateful for the cross. But should we be examining our gratitude more closely?

QUESTION 3: Interact with the following statement: "I am so thankful for Christ and the cross because it shows how valuable we must be to God."

Jonathan Edwards was a pastor in New England during the First Great Awakening. During these revivals, he saw many individuals make a profession of faith and declare their undying gratitude to God for salvation, only to fall away within a short time. As a result, he reflected deeply on the nature of true religious affections, including gratitude. In the following quotation, he writes about the gratitude of hypocrites.

> [Hypocrites] first rejoice, and are elevated with the fact that they are made much of by God; and then on that ground, [God] seems in a sort, lovely to them. . . . They are pleased in the highest degree, in hearing how much God and Christ make of them. So that their joy is really a joy in themselves, and not in God.[2]

Again, Edwards describes the joy of the hypocrite versus the joy of the saint.

> This is . . . the . . . difference between the joy of the hypocrite, and the joy of the true saint. The [hypocrite] rejoices in himself; self is the first foundation of his joy: the [true saint] rejoices in God. . . . True saints have their minds, in the first place, inexpressibly pleased and delighted in the sweet ideas of the glorious and amiable nature of the things of God. And this is the spring of all their delights, and the cream of all their pleasures. . . . But the dependence of the affections of hypocrites is in a contrary order: *they first rejoice . . . that they are made so much of by God; and then on that ground, he seems in a sort, lovely to them.*[3]

QUESTION 4: In your own words, what is the difference between the joy and gratitude of the hypocrite and the joy and gratitude of the saint? How might they look the same? How can we distinguish between them?

> Oh, that we would all heed the wisdom of Jonathan Edwards here. He is simply spelling out what it means to do all things—including giving thanks—to the glory of God (1 Cor. 10:31). He is showing us what the gospel is for. It is for the glory of God. And God is not glorified if the foundation of our gratitude for the gospel is the worth of its gifts and not the value of the Giver. If gratitude for the gospel is not rooted in the glory of God beneath the gift of God, it is disguised idolatry.[4]

DAY 3: DOES GOD DELIGHT IN US?

So far in this study, we have emphasized that God's love for us does not mean that he makes much of us, but rather that he frees us to enjoy making much of him forever. But is this the whole picture? Doesn't the Bible also speak of God delighting *in us*?

Study Isaiah 62:4-5, Zephaniah 3:17, and 1 Peter 1:6-7.

ISAIAH 62:4-5

> [4] *You shall no more be termed Forsaken, and your land shall no more be termed Desolate, but you shall be called My Delight Is in Her, and your land Married; for the LORD delights in you, and your land shall be married.* [5] *For as a young man marries a young woman, so shall your sons marry you, and as the bridegroom rejoices over the bride, so shall your God rejoice over you.*

ZEPHANIAH 3:17

> *The LORD your God is in your midst, a mighty one who will save; he will rejoice over you with gladness; he will quiet you by his love; he will exult over you with loud singing.*

1 PETER 1:6-7

> [6] *In this you rejoice, though now for a little while, if necessary, you have been grieved by various trials,* [7] *so that the tested genuineness of your faith—more precious than gold that perishes though it is tested by fire—may be found to result in praise and glory and honor at the revelation of Jesus Christ.*

QUESTION 5: In light of these texts, is it right to say that God does, in some sense, delight in and make much of us? If so, then for what reasons does God delight in us?

QUESTION 6: Attempt to reconcile the texts that teach that God delights in his people with the biblical truth that God does everything he does out of a supreme delight in himself. How can God delight in creatures without committing idolatry—that is, without putting other things before himself?

DAY 4: ENJOYING GOD'S ENJOYMENT OF US

In the last section, we saw that the Bible clearly tells us that God delights in his people. Moreover, one aspect of the hope of the Christian is that God will one day welcome us into his kingdom with the words, "Well done, good and faithful servant. . . . Enter into the joy of your master" (Matthew 25:21).

Read the following quotation from John Piper.

> The astonishing thing is that people . . . can become religious without being converted. That is, they join churches and start reading their Bibles and doing religious things, with no change in the foundation of their happiness. It is still themselves. They are the ground of their joy. Being made much of is the definition of love that they bring with them into the church. . . . Some churches are so misguided in their theology, they actually nurture that need and call it love. They interpret all the good feelings in the church as coming from the grace of God, when in fact natural principles can account for most of it.
>
> Other churches may not nurture the craving to be made much of, but unconverted people may interpret everything that is happening through that lens. So when the love of God is preached, they hear it to mean simply that God makes much of us. They may even have a strong affection for God as long as they see him as the endorsement of their delight in being the foundation of their own happiness. If God can be seen as the enabler of their self-exaltation, they will be happy to do some God-exaltation. If God is man-centered, they are willing to be, in a sense, God-centered.[5]

QUESTION 7: What great danger is present when we enjoy God's enjoyment of us? How can we ensure that we love praise from God ("Well done") for the right reasons?

Study Psalm 35:27 and Psalm 147:10-11.

PSALM 35:27

> Let those who delight in my righteousness shout for joy and be glad and say evermore, "Great is the LORD, who delights in the welfare of his servant!"

PSALM 147:10-11

> [10] His delight is not in the strength of the horse, nor his pleasure in the legs of a man, [11] but the LORD takes pleasure in those who fear him, in those who hope in his steadfast love.

QUESTION 8: Psalm 35:27 refers both to our delight in God and God's delight in us. According to this text, why do you think that God delights in us? Why does God delight in us according to Psalm 147:10-11?

God delights in the welfare of his servant because it shows his greatness. . . .

Hope turns fear into a trembling and peaceful wonder; and fear takes everything trivial out of hope and makes it earnest and profound. The terrors of God make the pleasures of his people intense. The fireside fellowship is all the sweeter when the storm is howling outside the cottage.

Now why does God delight in those who experience him in this way—in people who fear him and hope in his love?

Surely it is because our fear reflects the greatness of his power and our hope reflects the bounty of his grace. God delights in those responses which mirror his magnificence. This is just what we would have expected from a God who is all-sufficient in himself and has no need of us—a God who will never give up the glory of being the fountain of all joy, who will never surrender the honor of being the source of all safety, who will never abdicate the throne of sovereign grace. God has pleasure in those who hope in his love because that hope highlights the freedom of his grace. When I cry out, "God is my only hope, my rock, my refuge!" I am turning from myself and calling all attention to the boundless resources of God.[6]

DAY 5: DOES WORSHIP STROKE GOD'S EGO?

QUESTION 9: Respond to the following statement: "Why would God create creatures to worship him? Only petty tyrants crave praise from their people. If God is morally perfect, why would he need us to worship him?"

QUESTION 10: How would you explain the relationship between God's passion for his glory and God's love for us to a person who thought that God seems like an egomaniac?

FURTHER UP AND FURTHER IN

Read Chapter 7, "The Gospel—The Glory of the Gladness of God," in *God Is the Gospel* (pages 99-102).

QUESTION 11: Why is it so important that a great part of God's glory consists in his gladness? Why is the gladness of God good news for us?

Read Chapter 8, "The Gospel—The Glory of Christ as the Ground of Christ-Exalting Contrition," in *God Is the Gospel* (pages 106-115).

QUESTION 12: What is the relationship between genuine sorrow and repentance for sin and delight in the glory of God in the gospel? According to John Piper and Jonathan Edwards, which comes first? How should this truth affect our gospel proclamation?

QUESTION 13: According to John Piper, what is one reason that God allows Satan to remain alive and active in the world? Why does God not simply destroy him now?

Read Chapter 9, "The Gospel—The Glory of God Himself over and in All His Saving and Painful Gifts," in *God Is the Gospel* (pages 117-130).

QUESTION 14: Write out a biblical text that shows that God himself is the ultimate end of all of the following gospel gifts.

› Predestination
› Incarnation
› Reconciliation
› Consummation
› Eternal Life

On pages 127-129, John Piper discusses the following two texts from 2 Corinthians.

2 CORINTHIANS 1:8-9

[8] For we do not want you to be ignorant, brothers, of the afflic-tion we experienced in Asia. For we were so utterly burdened

beyond our strength that we despaired of life itself. [9] *Indeed, we felt that we had received the sentence of death. But that was to make us rely not on ourselves but on God who raises the dead.*

2 CORINTHIANS 12:7-10

[7] *So to keep me from being too elated by the surpassing greatness of the revelations, a thorn was given me in the flesh, a messenger of Satan to harass me, to keep me from becoming conceited.* [8] *Three times I pleaded with the Lord about this, that it should leave me.* [9] *But he said to me, "My grace is sufficient for you, for my power is made perfect in weakness." Therefore I will boast all the more gladly of my weaknesses, so that the power of Christ may rest upon me.* [10] *For the sake of Christ, then, I am content with weaknesses, insults, hardships, persecutions, and calamities. For when I am weak, then I am strong.*

QUESTION 15: What was God's design in both of these difficult situations? How did God's design differ from the design of those threatening Paul's life in 2 Corinthians 1:8-9 and the design of Satan's messenger in 2 Corinthians 12:7-10? How does this provide us with incredible encouragement when we suffer affliction?

WHILE YOU WATCH THE DVD, TAKE NOTES

What is the key difference between the joy of the saint and the joy of the hypocrite?

What is a key problem with many modern evangelistic strategies?

What is John Piper's answer to the question, "Why does God rejoice over us?"

Why does God tell us that he delights in us?

Summarize John Piper's response to Michael Prowse.

AFTER YOU WATCH THE DVD, DISCUSS WHAT YOU'VE LEARNED

1) Discuss ways to identify idolatrous gratitude in your own life and in the life of your church. How can you avoid idolatrous gratitude?

2) How would you answer the question, "Does God like us?"

3) Discuss Michael Prowse's criticism of the worship of God. What key fact is Prowse overlooking?

AFTER YOU DISCUSS, MAKE APPLICATION

1) What was the most meaningful part of this lesson for you? Was there a sentence, concept, or idea that really struck you? Why? Record your thoughts in the space below.

2) Memorize Psalm 147:10-11 this week. Spend at least ten minutes meditating on God's delight in those who fear him and hope in his steadfast love. Record your reflections below.

NOTES

1. Excerpt taken from an online sermon at the Desiring God web site entitled, "Proud People Don't Say Thanks." Throughout this study guide, articles and sermons at the Desiring God web site (www.desiringGod.org) may be found by performing a title search on the home page.
2. As quoted in *God Is the Gospel*, page 137.
3. Excerpt taken from *God Is the Gospel*, page 150.
4. Excerpt taken from *God Is the Gospel*, pages 137-138.
5. Excerpt taken from *God Is the Gospel*, pages 149-150.
6. Excerpt taken from *The Pleasures of God*, pages 186, 199.

LESSON 6
THE GOSPEL: EVENT, ACCOMPLISHMENT, AND OFFER
A Companion Study to the God Is the Gospel DVD, Session 5

LESSON OBJECTIVES

It is our prayer that after you have finished this lesson . . .

> ❯ You will understand the many different ways of looking at the gospel.
> ❯ You will grow in your understanding of the glorious blessings that Christ has accomplished for us.
> ❯ You will understand why faith is indispensable to becoming a partaker in the gospel.

BEFORE YOU WATCH THE DVD, STUDY AND PREPARE

DAY 1: WHAT IS THE GOSPEL?

The final two lessons will explore the relationship between the statement "God is the gospel" and more traditional statements of the gospel of Jesus Christ. The Bible offers us many descriptions of "the gospel." In the following quotation, John Piper explains the difficulty in defining "the gospel."

> The challenge in defining such a common and broad word or phrase like "good news" or "declare good news" is to avoid two extremes. One extreme would be to define the Christian gospel so broadly that everything good in the Christian message is called gospel, and the other would be to define the Christian gospel so narrowly that the definition cannot do justice to all the uses in the New Testament.[1]

The roots of the meaning of the word "gospel" in the New Testament lie in the Old Testament.

Study Isaiah 40:9 and Isaiah 52:7.

ISAIAH 40:9

Get you up to a high mountain, O Zion, herald of good news; lift up your voice with strength, O Jerusalem, herald of good news; lift it up, fear not; say to the cities of Judah, "Behold your God!"

ISAIAH 52:7

How beautiful upon the mountains are the feet of him who brings good news, who publishes peace, who brings good news of happiness, who publishes salvation, who says to Zion, "Your God reigns."

QUESTION 1: Summarize the essence of the gospel from these passages.

While the Old Testament laid the foundation for the gospel, the fullness of its meaning is revealed in the New Testament.

Study 1 Corinthians 15:1-4 and Galatians 4:4-6.

1 CORINTHIANS 15:1-4

[1] Now I would remind you, brothers, of the gospel I preached to you, which you received, in which you stand, [2] and by which you are being saved, if you hold fast to the word I preached to you—unless you believed in vain. [3] For I delivered to you as of first importance what I also received: that Christ died for our sins in accordance with the Scriptures, [4] that he was buried, that he was raised on the third day in accordance with the Scriptures.

GALATIANS 4:4-6

[4] But when the fullness of time had come, God sent forth his Son, born of woman, born under the law, [5] to redeem those who were under the law, so that we might receive adoption as sons. [6] And because you are sons, God has sent the Spirit of his Son into our hearts, crying, "Abba! Father!"

QUESTION 2: Summarize the content of the gospel from these two passages. What are the key elements that Paul mentions here?

DAY 2: THE GOSPEL AND GOD'S WRATH

In the last section, you studied the events that make up the good news. But the gospel is not merely events. John Piper explains this crucial point.

> But the gospel is not only news. It is first news, and then it is doctrine. *Doctrine* means teaching, explaining, clarifying. Doctrine is part of the gospel because news can't be just declared by the mouth of the herald—it has to be understood in the mind of a hearer. . . . When the gospel is proclaimed, it must be explained. . . .
>
> Gospel doctrine matters because the good news is so full and rich and wonderful that it must be opened like a treasure chest, and all its treasures brought out for the enjoyment of the world. Doctrine is the description of these treasures. Doctrine describes their true value and why they are so valuable. Doctrine guards the diamonds of the gospel from being discarded as mere crystals. Doctrine protects the treasures of the gospel from pirates who don't like the diamonds but who make their living trading them for other stones. Doctrine polishes the old gems buried at the bottom of the chest. It puts the jewels of gospel truth in order on the scarlet tapestry of history so each is seen in its most beautiful place.[2]

Study Galatians 3:13-14, 1 Thessalonians 1:9-10, and John 3:36.

GALATIANS 3:13-14

> [13] *Christ redeemed us from the curse of the law by becoming a curse for us—for it is written, "Cursed is everyone who is hanged on a tree"—*[14] *so that in Christ Jesus the blessing of*

Abraham might come to the Gentiles, so that we might receive the promised Spirit through faith.

1 THESSALONIANS 1:9-10

⁹ For they themselves report concerning us the kind of reception we had among you, and how you turned to God from idols to serve the living and true God, ¹⁰ and to wait for his Son from heaven, whom he raised from the dead, Jesus who delivers us from the wrath to come.

JOHN 3:36

³⁶ Whoever believes in the Son has eternal life; whoever does not obey the Son shall not see life, but the wrath of God remains on him.

QUESTION 3: What is the chief accomplishment of the gospel in these passages? How did Christ bring about this accomplishment?

The justification of sinners is one of the biggest problems in the universe. John Piper lays out the essence of this problem.

Justice proceeds on the principle laid down in Proverbs 17:15, "He who justifies the wicked and he who condemns the righteous are both alike an abomination to the LORD." We impeach judges who acquit the guilty. Our moral sensibility is outraged when wrong is given legal sanction. Yet at the heart of the Christian gospel stands the sentence: God justifies the ungodly (Romans 4:5). He acquits the guilty. That is the gospel. But how can it be right for God to do that?[3]

Study the following passage.

ROMANS 3:23-26

[23] *For all have sinned and fall short of the glory of God,* [24] *and are justified by his grace as a gift, through the redemption that is in Christ Jesus,* [25] *whom God put forward as a propitiation by his blood, to be received by faith. This was to show God's righteousness, because in his divine forbearance he had passed over former sins.* [26] *It was to show his righteousness at the present time, so that he might be just and the justifier of the one who has faith in Jesus.*

QUESTION 4: How does this passage solve the problem created by God's justification of the ungodly? How is God able to be both just and the justifier of the ungodly person who has faith in Jesus?

DAY 3: THE GOSPEL AND SIN

The last section centered on the removal of God's wrath through the cross of Christ. This lesson will focus on a related blessing of the gospel.

Study the following passage.

ISAIAH 53

[1] *Who has believed what he has heard from us? And to whom has the arm of the LORD been revealed?* [2] *For he grew up before him like a young plant, and like a root out of dry ground; he had no form or majesty that we should look at him, and no beauty that we should desire him.* [3] *He was despised and rejected by men; a man of sorrows, and acquainted with grief; and as one from whom men hide their faces he was despised, and we esteemed him not.* [4] *Surely he has borne our griefs and carried our sorrows; yet we esteemed him stricken, smitten by God, and afflicted.* [5] *But he was wounded for our transgressions; he was crushed for our iniquities; upon him was the chastisement that brought us peace, and with his stripes we are healed.* [6] *All we like sheep have gone astray; we have turned—every one—to his own way; and the LORD has laid on him the iniquity of us all.* [7] *He was oppressed, and he was afflicted, yet he opened not his mouth; like a lamb that is led to the slaughter, and like a sheep that before its shearers is silent, so he opened not his mouth.* [8] *By oppression and judgment he was taken away; and as for his generation, who considered that he was cut off out of the land of the living, stricken for the transgression of my people?* [9] *And they made his grave with the wicked and with a rich man in his death, although he had done no violence, and there was no deceit in his mouth.* [10] *Yet it was the will of the LORD to crush him; he has put him to grief; when his soul makes an offering for guilt, he shall see his offspring; he shall prolong his days; the will of the LORD shall prosper in his hand.* [11] *Out of the anguish of his soul he shall see and be satisfied; by his knowledge shall the righteous one, my servant, make many to be accounted righteous, and he shall bear their iniquities.* [12] *Therefore I will divide him a portion with the many, and he shall divide the spoil with the strong, because he poured out his soul to death and was numbered with the transgressors; yet he bore the sin of many, and makes intercession for the transgressors.*

QUESTION 5: Underline every phrase that prophetically speaks of the cross of Christ. What is the central accomplishment of the cross in this passage?

This is a prophecy and picture of Jesus Christ crucified and raised from the dead hundreds of years before it happens. The *bruising* is the crucifixion and death of Jesus, making himself an offering for sin. It is a bruising unto death. This is confirmed in Isaiah 53:8, "He was cut off out of the land of the living . . . they made his grave with the wicked." And again in verse 12: "He poured out his soul to death." The reference to *prolonging his days*, on the other hand, is a reference to Christ's resurrection to eternal life after death. This is confirmed in verse 12 by the prophecy that God will "divide him a portion with the great" even though he had already died. And when it says that he will see his *offspring*, it means that the fruit of his suffering will be many people saved from sin and death. This is confirmed in verse 11: "He shall see the fruit of the travail of his soul and be satisfied; by his knowledge shall the righteous one, my servant, make many accounted righteous; and he shall bear their iniquities."[4]

The significance of Isaiah 53 was not lost on the early church. Peter connects the ancient prophecy to the work of Christ in 1 Peter 2.

Study the following passage.

1 PETER 2:22-25

> [22] *He committed no sin, neither was deceit found in his mouth.* [23] *When he was reviled, he did not revile in return; when he suffered, he did not threaten, but continued entrusting himself to him who judges justly.* [24] *He himself bore our sins in his body on the tree, that we might die to sin and live to righteousness. By his wounds you have been healed.* [25] *For you were straying like sheep, but have now returned to the Shepherd and Overseer of your souls.*

QUESTION 6: Underline every phrase that is derived from Isaiah 53. How does Peter describe the purpose of the cross in this passage?

DAY 4: RIGHTEOUSNESS AND LIFE

We have seen that Christ bore our sins on the cross. But is this all that was necessary? Yes, our sins have been forgiven. But justification is not the same as forgiveness. Forgiveness means that you don't have sin applied to your account. Justification means that you do have righteousness applied to your account.

Study the following passage.

ROMANS 5:12-21

> [12] *Therefore, just as sin came into the world through one man, and death through sin, and so death spread to all men because all sinned—* [13] *for sin indeed was in the world before the law was*

given, but sin is not counted where there is no law. [14] *Yet death reigned from Adam to Moses, even over those whose sinning was not like the transgression of Adam, who was a type of the one who was to come.* [15] *But the free gift is not like the trespass. For if many died through one man's trespass, much more have the grace of God and the free gift by the grace of that one man Jesus Christ abounded for many.* [16] *And the free gift is not like the result of that one man's sin. For the judgment following one trespass brought condemnation, but the free gift following many trespasses brought justification.* [17] *If, because of one man's trespass, death reigned through that one man, much more will those who receive the abundance of grace and the free gift of righteousness reign in life through the one man Jesus Christ.* [18] *Therefore, as one trespass led to condemnation for all men, so one act of righteousness leads to justification and life for all men.* [19] *For as by the one man's disobedience the many were made sinners, so by the one man's obedience the many will be made righteous.* [20] *Now the law came in to increase the trespass, but where sin increased, grace abounded all the more,* [21] *so that, as sin reigned in death, grace also might reign through righteousness leading to eternal life through Jesus Christ our Lord.*

QUESTION 7: What comparison and contrast does Paul draw in this passage? According to verse 19, how will the many be made righteous? Summarize the main point of this passage in your own words.

To make a way for us to be saved, God sent Christ to live a perfect divine-human life and die an obedient death. In this way Christ became both the substitute punishment for our sins (Matt. 26:28; 1 Cor. 15:3; 1 Pet. 3:18) and the substitute performer of our righteousness (Rom. 5:19; 10:4;

2 Cor. 5:21; Phil. 3:9). Therefore, in the courtroom of God, my guilt for sin is removed by Christ's blood ("In him we have redemption through his blood, the forgiveness of our trespasses" [Eph. 1:7]); and my title to heaven is provided by Christ's obedience ("By the one man's obedience the many will be made righteous" [Rom. 5:19]). I am declared just—freed from the punishment of sin and now possessing a title to heaven. This is what we mean by justification.[5]

John 3:16 is one of the most beloved passages in all of Scripture. Study the following passage.

JOHN 3:16

For God so loved the world, that he gave his only Son, that whoever believes in him should not perish but have eternal life.

QUESTION 8: Identify four aspects of the gospel in this verse. What is the purpose of the cross according to John 3:16?

DAY 5: THE OFFER OF THE GOSPEL

So far in this lesson, we have focused on the gospel events and what they accomplished. But if all we have are events and accomplishments with no way to become a partaker of them, then the gospel is not good news. In this final section we will examine the means by which we come into possession of the benefits of the gospel.

Study Acts 2:37-38, Acts 16:30-31, Galatians 2:16, and John 6:35.

ACTS 2:37-38

> 37 Now when they heard this they were cut to the heart, and said to Peter and the rest of the apostles, "Brothers, what shall we do?" 38 And Peter said to them, "Repent and be baptized every one of you in the name of Jesus Christ for the forgiveness of your sins, and you will receive the gift of the Holy Spirit."

ACTS 16:30-31

> 30 Then he brought them out and said, "Sirs, what must I do to be saved?" 31 And they said, "Believe in the Lord Jesus, and you will be saved, you and your household."

GALATIANS 2:16

> We know that a person is not justified by works of the law but through faith in Jesus Christ, so we also have believed in Christ Jesus, in order to be justified by faith in Christ and not by works of the law, because by works of the law no one will be justified.

JOHN 6:35

> Jesus said to them, "I am the bread of life; whoever comes to me shall not hunger, and whoever believes in me shall never thirst."

QUESTION 9: According to these passages, how do we become connected to Christ and the benefits he accomplished in the gospel? Then, using John 6:35, provide your own definition of faith.

Study Ephesians 2:8-10 and Romans 4:19-21.

EPHESIANS 2:8-10

⁸ For by grace you have been saved through faith. And this is not your own doing; it is the gift of God, ⁹ not a result of works, so that no one may boast. ¹⁰ For we are his workmanship, created in Christ Jesus for good works, which God prepared beforehand, that we should walk in them.

ROMANS 4:19-21

¹⁹ [Abraham] did not weaken in faith when he considered his own body, which was as good as dead (since he was about a hundred years old), or when he considered the barrenness of Sarah's womb. ²⁰ No distrust made him waver concerning the promise of God, but he grew strong in his faith as he gave glory to God, ²¹ fully convinced that God was able to do what he had promised.

QUESTION 10: According to these texts, why is it important that we are saved by grace through faith? What would happen if we were saved by our works?

The New Testament correlates faith and grace to make sure that we do not boast in what grace alone achieves. One of the most familiar examples goes like this: "For by *grace* you have been saved through *faith*" (Ephesians 2:8). By *grace*, through *faith*. There's the correlation that guards the freedom of grace. Faith is the act of our soul that turns away

from our own insufficiency to the free and all-sufficient resources of God. Faith focuses on the freedom of God to
dispense grace to the unworthy. It banks on the bounty of
God.

Therefore faith, by its very nature, nullifies boasting and fits
with grace. Wherever faith looks, it sees grace behind every
praiseworthy act. So it cannot boast, except in the Lord. So
Paul, after saying that salvation is by grace through faith,
says, ". . . and that not of yourselves, it is the gift of God; not
as a result of works, *that no one should boast*" (Ephesians
2:8-9). Faith cannot boast in human goodness or compe-
tence or wisdom, because faith focuses on the free, all-
supplying grace of God. Whatever goodness faith sees, it
sees as the fruit of grace.[6]

FURTHER UP AND FURTHER IN

Read Chapter 10, "The Gospel—The Gift of God Himself
over and in All His Pleasant Gifts," in *God Is the Gospel* (pages
133-145).

QUESTION 11: Where do answers to prayer come from?
Cite Scripture in your answer. Why is it important to keep in mind
the costly ground of answered prayer?

QUESTION 12: In your own words, summarize how it is
possible to enjoy all of God's good gifts without becoming an
idolater. What is the difference between the way that an unbeliever enjoys creation and the way that a believer enjoys creation?

Why must we emphasize this difference when speaking of the gospel?

Read Chapter 11, "The Gospel—What Makes It Ultimately Good: Seeing Glory or Being Glorious?" in *God Is the Gospel* (pages 147-162).

QUESTION 13: After reading this chapter, define *conversion* in your own words. How does this understanding of conversion differ from other descriptions of conversion that you have heard?

QUESTION 14: On pages 159-160, John Piper provides a number of questions to determine whether our desire to be like Christ is ultimately honoring to God. Spend time reflecting on these questions and your own heart. Record your reflections below.

QUESTION 15: In this chapter, John Piper speaks of seeing God, being like God, savoring God, and displaying God.

How should we connect these four aspects of the ultimate end of the gospel? How will these four realities manifest themselves in eternity?

WHILE YOU WATCH THE DVD, TAKE NOTES

What are the five ways that we can describe the gospel?

1)

2)

3)

4)

5)

If _____ isn't _____, we _____.

What passage of Scripture did John Piper memorize as a boy?

Why is the obedience of Jesus important for the gospel?

What requirement would make the gospel offer into bad news?

AFTER YOU WATCH THE DVD, DISCUSS WHAT YOU'VE LEARNED

1) Discuss the five ways that John Piper describes the gospel. Which of these are you most accustomed to hearing when you hear the word *gospel*?

2) Why is it important to preserve the obedience of Jesus when we talk about the gospel? What is lost if we only refer to the sin-bearing work of Christ and not the law-fulfilling work of Christ?

3) John Piper briefly discussed the relationship between Romans 5 and 6. How do some people distort the

teaching that we receive eternal life as a gift of grace? What wrong conclusion do they draw?

AFTER YOU DISCUSS, MAKE APPLICATION

1) What was the most meaningful part of this lesson for you? Was there a sentence, concept, or idea that really struck you? Why? Record your thoughts in the space below.

2) Choose one of the accomplishments of the gospel that you studied this week and share it with someone else. Explain to them the significance of this accomplishment for the good news. Record your reflections on this conversation below.

NOTES

1. Excerpt taken from *God Is the Gospel*, page 26.
2. Excerpt taken from *God Is the Gospel*, pages 21-22.
3. Excerpt taken from *The Pleasures of God*, pages 162-163.
4. Excerpt taken from *The Pleasures of God*, page 160.
5. Excerpt taken from *When I Don't Desire God*, page 83.
6. Excerpt taken from *Future Grace*, page 186.

LESSON 7
THE GOSPEL: APPLICATION AND BEYOND
A Companion Study to the God Is the Gospel DVD, Session 6

LESSON OBJECTIVES

It is our prayer that after you have finished this lesson . . .

> You will follow all the blessings of the gospel to their highest and deepest point and see what ultimately makes the good news good.

> You will glorify God for his sovereignty in bringing you from darkness to light.

> You will be stunned by the greatness of God in and through all of his glorious gifts.

BEFORE YOU WATCH THE DVD, STUDY AND PREPARE

DAY 1: WHAT MAKES THE GOOD NEWS GOOD?

In the last lesson we explored various accomplishments of the gospel. Because of the gospel, God's wrath is removed, our sins are forgiven, a perfect righteousness has been performed for us, and eternal life has been provided. All of these blessings are offered to us solely by faith in Jesus Christ. In this lesson, we will seek to determine what makes each of these blessings "good news."

Study the following passage.

ROMANS 5:1-11

1 Therefore, since we have been justified by faith, we have peace with God through our Lord Jesus Christ. 2 Through him we have also obtained access by faith into this grace in which we stand, and we rejoice in hope of the glory of God. 3 More than that, we rejoice in our sufferings, knowing that suffering produces endurance, 4 and endurance produces character, and character produces hope, 5 and hope does not put us to shame, because God's love has been poured into our hearts through the Holy Spirit who has been given to us. 6 For while we were still weak, at the right time Christ died for the ungodly. 7 For one will scarcely die for a righteous person—though perhaps for a good person one would dare even to die— 8 but God shows his love for us in that while we were still sinners, Christ died for us. 9 Since, therefore, we have now been justified by his blood, much more shall we be saved by him from the wrath of God. 10 For if while we were enemies we were reconciled to God by the death of his Son, much more, now that we are reconciled, shall we be saved by his life. 11 More than that, we also rejoice in God through our Lord Jesus Christ, through whom we have now received reconciliation.

QUESTION 1: Look closely at Romans 5:1-3. According to this text, why is the provision of perfect righteousness that we receive in justification good news? Why would anyone want to be justified?

QUESTION 2: Now examine Romans 5:9-11. Why is it good news that God's wrath has been removed from us? Be specific.

> The aim of reconciliation is not safe and sullen solidarity. The aim is that we "rejoice in God through our Lord Jesus Christ." God is the focus of the reconciliation. The joy of reconciliation is joy in God. Therefore, when we preach the gospel of reconciliation, the focus must not be merely the removal of enmity, but the arrival of joy in God.[1]

DAY 2: WHAT IS ETERNAL LIFE?

> Eternal life is one of the most treasured gifts of the gospel. It is rooted in one of the most familiar and best-loved gospel promises, John 3:16: "For God so loved the world, that he gave his only Son, that whoever believes in him should not perish but have *eternal life*." So the promise of eternal life is connected to the love of God and the gift of his Son. What then is this gift that flows from the gospel and from the love of God?[2]

Study the following passage.

JOHN 17:1-5

[1] *When Jesus had spoken these words, he lifted up his eyes to heaven, and said, "Father, the hour has come; glorify your Son that the Son may glorify you,* [2] *since you have given him authority over all flesh, to give eternal life to all whom you have given*

him. ³ *And this is eternal life, that they know you the only true God, and Jesus Christ whom you have sent.* ⁴ *I glorified you on earth, having accomplished the work that you gave me to do.* ⁵ *And now, Father, glorify me in your own presence with the glory that I had with you before the world existed."*

QUESTION 3: How does Jesus define eternal life in this passage? What is the relationship between eternal life and the glory of God?

John 17:1-5 is the beginning of Jesus' final prayer for his disciples before he was crucified. You have seen that this prayer is God-centered from the very beginning. But not only does it begin in a God-centered manner, it ends in a similar way.

Study the following passage.

JOHN 17:24-26

²⁴ *Father, I desire that they also, whom you have given me, may be with me where I am, to see my glory that you have given me because you loved me before the foundation of the world.* ²⁵ *O righteous Father, even though the world does not know you, I know you, and these know that you have sent me.* ²⁶ *I made known to them your name, and I will continue to make it known, that the love with which you have loved me may be in them, and I in them.*

QUESTION 4: What is Jesus' great desire in this prayer? How does this relate to "God is the gospel"?

[W]hen we share in the happiness of God we share in the very pleasure that the Father has in the Son. This is why Jesus made the Father known to us. . . . He made God known so that God's pleasure in his Son might be in us and become our pleasure.

Imagine being able to enjoy what is most enjoyable with unbounded energy and passion forever. This is not now our experience. . . .

But if the aim of Jesus in John 17:26 comes true, all this will change. If God's pleasure in the Son becomes our pleasure, then the object of our pleasure, Jesus, will be inexhaustible in personal worth. He will never become boring or disappointing or frustrating. No greater treasure can be conceived than the Son of God. Moreover, our ability to savor this inexhaustible treasure will not be limited by human weaknesses. We will enjoy the Son of God with the very enjoyment of his Father. God's delight in his Son will be in us and it will be ours.[3]

DAY 3: FROM DARKNESS TO LIGHT

In one sense, this study is an extended meditation on the truth expressed in 2 Corinthians 4:4-6. In this text Paul describes the gospel as "the gospel of the glory of Christ, who is the image of God."

Study the following passage.

2 CORINTHIANS 4:4-6

[4] *In their case the god of this world has blinded the minds of the unbelievers, to keep them from seeing the light of the gospel of the glory of Christ, who is the image of God.* [5] *For what we proclaim is not ourselves, but Jesus Christ as Lord, with*

ourselves as your servants for Jesus' sake. ⁶ *For God, who said,*
"Let light shine out of darkness," has shone in our hearts to
give the light of the knowledge of the glory of God in the face
of Jesus Christ.

QUESTION 5: How does verse 4 describe the natural state of human beings? What is the remedy to this problem? What contrast does Paul make in verse 6?

"God, who said, 'Let light shine out of darkness,' has shone in our hearts to give the light of the knowledge of the glory of God in the face of Jesus Christ." This means that in the dark and troubled heart of unbelief, God does what he did in the dark and unformed creation at the beginning of our world. He said, "Let there be light," and there was light. So he says to the blind and dark heart, "Let there be light," and there is light in the heart of the sinner. In this light we see the glory of God in the face of Christ. . . . In verse 4 Satan blinds the mind; in verse 6 God creates light in the heart. Verse 4 describes the problem; verse 6 describes the remedy. These two verses are a description of the condition of all people before conversion, and what happens in conversion to bring about salvation. More than any part of the Bible that I know of, the connections between 2 Corinthians 4:4 and 6 shed light on the ultimate meaning of *good* in the term *good news.*⁴

QUESTION 6: If conversion is compared to a sovereign work of new creation on God's part, are human messengers irrelevant in sinners coming to see and savor the glory of God in the face of Christ? In other words, does the sovereignty of God in the creation of gospel light remove the need for human messengers? Explain your answer from 2 Corinthians 4:4-6.

DAY 4: ECHOES OF GLORY FOR ALL TO SEE

At this point in the study you may be wondering, "If the ultimate good of the gospel is God himself, and unbelievers are blinded so they cannot see the glory of God in the gospel, how will sinners ever come to desire the gospel? Are there any connections between unbelievers and the glory of God in the gospel?"

QUESTION 7: Every year thousands of people venture to the Grand Canyon, the Rocky Mountains, and other natural wonders. Speculate on why they go to such places. What is so enjoyable about seeing the great wonders of creation?

QUESTION 8: Every year millions of people go to sports events to watch athletes who play the game better than they do. They watch movies and television shows in which the actors act better than they can. Why do people pay money to watch individuals do things better than they can? How might this relate to "God is the gospel"?

DAY 5: GOD IS THE GREATEST GIFT OF THE GOSPEL

Perhaps no one outside of the biblical authors has thought more deeply and clearly about the relationship of God to every joy in life than Jonathan Edwards. Read the following quotation from Jonathan Edwards's sermon "God Glorified in the Work of Redemption."

> The redeemed have all their objective good in God. God himself is the great good which they are brought to the possession and enjoyment of by redemption. He is the highest good, and the sum of all that good which Christ purchased. God is the inheritance of the saints; he is the portion of their souls. God is their wealth and treasure, their food, their life, their dwelling place, their ornament and diadem, and their everlasting honor and glory. They have none in heaven but God; he is the great good which the redeemed are received to at death, and which they are to rise to at the end of the world. The Lord God, he is the light of the heavenly Jerusalem; and is the 'river of the water of life' that runs, and the tree of life that grows, 'in the midst of the paradise of God'. The glorious excellencies and beauty of God will be what will forever entertain the minds of the saints, and the love of God will be their everlasting feast. The redeemed will

indeed enjoy other things; they will enjoy the angels, and will enjoy one another: but that which they shall enjoy in the angels, or each other, or in anything else whatsoever, that will yield them delight and happiness, will be what will be seen of God in them.[5]

QUESTION 9: Reflect on this quotation from Jonathan Edwards. Record any thoughts or reactions in the space below.

In the quotation above, Jonathan Edwards alludes to the great scene at the end of the book of Revelation concerning the new heavens and new earth.

Study the following passage.

REVELATION 21:1–22:5

[1] Then I saw a new heaven and a new earth, for the first heaven and the first earth had passed away, and the sea was no more. [2] And I saw the holy city, new Jerusalem, coming down out of heaven from God, prepared as a bride adorned for her husband. [3] And I heard a loud voice from the throne saying, "Behold, the dwelling place of God is with man. He will dwell with them, and they will be his people, and God himself will be with them as their God. [4] He will wipe away every tear from their eyes, and death shall be no more, neither shall there be mourning, nor crying, nor pain anymore, for the former things have passed away." [5] And he who was seated on the throne said, "Behold, I am making all things new." Also he said, "Write this down, for these words are trustworthy and true." [6] And he said to me, "It is done! I am the Alpha and the Omega, the beginning and

the end. To the thirsty I will give from the spring of the water of life without payment. [7] The one who conquers will have this heritage, and I will be his God and he will be my son. [8] But as for the cowardly, the faithless, the detestable, as for murderers, the sexually immoral, sorcerers, idolaters, and all liars, their portion will be in the lake that burns with fire and sulfur, which is the second death." [9] Then came one of the seven angels who had the seven bowls full of the seven last plagues and spoke to me, saying, "Come, I will show you the Bride, the wife of the Lamb." [10] And he carried me away in the Spirit to a great, high mountain, and showed me the holy city Jerusalem coming down out of heaven from God, [11] having the glory of God, its radiance like a most rare jewel, like a jasper, clear as crystal. [12] It had a great, high wall, with twelve gates, and at the gates twelve angels, and on the gates the names of the twelve tribes of the sons of Israel were inscribed—[13] on the east three gates, on the north three gates, on the south three gates, and on the west three gates. [14] And the wall of the city had twelve foundations, and on them were the twelve names of the twelve apostles of the Lamb. [15] And the one who spoke with me had a measuring rod of gold to measure the city and its gates and walls. [16] The city lies foursquare, its length the same as its width. And he measured the city with his rod, 12,000 stadia. Its length and width and height are equal. [17] He also measured its wall, 144 cubits by human measurement, which is also an angel's measurement. [18] The wall was built of jasper, while the city was pure gold, clear as glass. [19] The foundations of the wall of the city were adorned with every kind of jewel. The first was jasper, the second sapphire, the third agate, the fourth emerald, [20] the fifth onyx, the sixth carnelian, the seventh chrysolite, the eighth beryl, the ninth topaz, the tenth chrysoprase, the eleventh jacinth, the twelfth amethyst. [21] And the twelve gates were twelve pearls, each of the gates made of a single pearl, and the street of the city was pure gold, transparent as glass. [22] And I saw no temple in the city, for its temple is the Lord God the Almighty and the Lamb. [23] And the city has no need of sun or moon to shine on it, for the glory of God gives it light, and its lamp is the Lamb. [24] By its light will the nations walk, and the kings of the earth will bring their glory into it, [25] and its gates will never be shut by day—and there will be no night there. [26] They will bring into it the glory and the honor of the nations. ²⁷ *But nothing unclean will ever enter it, nor anyone who does what is detestable or false, but only those who are written in the Lamb's book of life.*

^{22:1} *Then the angel showed me the river of the water of life, bright as crystal, flowing from the throne of God and of the Lamb* ² *through the middle of the street of the city; also, on either side of the river, the tree of life with its twelve kinds of fruit, yielding its fruit each month. The leaves of the tree were for the healing of the nations.* ³ *No longer will there be anything accursed, but the throne of God and of the Lamb will be in it, and his servants will worship him.* ⁴ *They will see his face, and his name will be on their foreheads.* ⁵ *And night will be no more. They will need no light of lamp or sun, for the Lord God will be their light, and they will reign forever and ever.*

QUESTION 10: Underline every phrase in this passage that implies that God is the great good of the new heavens and the new earth. Record your reflections on this passage below.

FURTHER UP AND FURTHER IN

Read the Conclusion, "God Is the Gospel—Now Let Us Sacrifice and Sing," in *God Is the Gospel* (pages 165-179).

QUESTION 11: On pages 165-167, John Piper summarizes the argument of this book. In a short paragraph, offer your own summary of the content of the book.

QUESTION 12: Give three practical ways that our proclamation of the gospel will be affected by the truth that "God is the gospel."

QUESTION 13: Give three practical ways that your own sanctification will be affected by the truth that "God is the gospel."

QUESTION 14: Choose one of the songs on pages 170-173 and reflect on the words. How does this song make clear that "God is the gospel"? Record any new insights that you have after reading this song.

QUESTION 15: Choose one of the songs on pages 173-179 and reflect on the words. How does this song make clear that

"God is the gospel"? Record any new insights that you have after reading this song.

WHILE YOU WATCH THE DVD, TAKE NOTES

What story does John Piper use to illustrate what is "good" about forgiveness?

Paul describes _____ as _____ to _____.

According to John Piper, why do unbelievers go to the Grand Canyon and to sporting events?

What brief answer does John Piper give to the question, "How do I become more like this?"

How can we make God's glory visible in the world?

AFTER YOU WATCH THE DVD, DISCUSS WHAT YOU'VE LEARNED

1) Why is it important to continually ask for the reason why the benefits of the gospel are good news? Why is it dangerous to simply focus on these good gifts and not ask why they are good?

2) Why is it freeing to know that God is the one who causes light to shine out of the darkness in the heart of an unbeliever?

3) Discuss other examples of common ground that you could build between unbelievers to help them see why they were made.

AFTER YOU DISCUSS, MAKE APPLICATION

1) What was the most meaningful part of this lesson for you? Was there a sentence, concept, or idea that really struck you? Why? Record your thoughts in the space below.

2) Pray this week for an unbeliever whom you know. Pray that God would cause light to shine in his or her heart. Then seek an opportunity to build common ground with him or her by asking about his or her desire to see and admire greatness in the world. Record the results of your conversation below.

NOTES

1. Excerpt taken from *God Is the Gospel*, page 120.
2. Excerpt taken from *God Is the Gospel*, page 123.
3. Excerpt taken from *The Pleasures of God*, pages 26-27.
4. Excerpt taken from *God Is the Gospel*, page 61.
5. As quoted in *God Is the Gospel*, page 145.

LESSON 8
REVIEW AND CONCLUSION

LESSON OBJECTIVES

It is our prayer that after you have finished this lesson . . .

> You will be able to summarize and synthesize what you've learned.

> You will hear what others in your group have learned.

> You will share with others how you have begun to see the gospel in a new light.

WHAT HAVE YOU LEARNED?

There are no study questions to answer in preparation for this lesson. Instead, spend your time writing a few paragraphs that explain what you've learned in this group study. To help you do this, you may choose to review the notes you've taken in the previous lessons. Then, after you've written down what you've learned, write down some questions that still remain in your mind about anything addressed in these lessons. Be prepared to share these reflections and questions with the group in the next lesson.

NOTES

Use this space to record anything in the group discussion that you want to remember:

LEADER'S GUIDE

AS THE LEADER OF THIS GROUP STUDY, *it is imperative that you are completely familiar with this study guide* and with the *God Is the Gospel* DVD Set. Therefore, it is our strong recommendation that you (1) read and understand the introduction, (2) skim each lesson, surveying its layout and content, and (3) read the entire Leader's Guide *before* you begin the group study and distribute the study guides. As you review this Leader's Guide, keep in mind that the material here is only a recommendation. As the leader of the study, feel free to adapt this study guide to your situation and context.

BEFORE LESSON 1

Before the first lesson, you will need to know approximately how many participants you will have in your group study. *Each participant will need his or her own study guide!* Therefore, be sure to order enough study guides. You will distribute these study guides at the beginning of the first lesson.

It is also our strong recommendation that you, as the leader, familiarize yourself with this study guide and the *God Is the Gospel* DVD Set in order to answer any questions that might arise and also to ensure that each group session runs smoothly and maximizes the learning of the participants. It is not necessary for you to preview *God Is the Gospel* in its entirety—although it certainly wouldn't hurt!—but you should be prepared to navigate your way through each DVD menu.

NOTE: As we noted in the Introduction, this study guide is designed for an eight-session guided study. However, we understand that there are times when a group may only have six weeks with which to complete this study. In such a case, we recommend abbreviating Lesson 1 and completing it along with Lesson 2 in the first week. The preparatory work for Lesson 2 can be completed as a group during the first session. In addition, Lesson 8 may be completed by students on their own after the group has met for the final time.

DURING LESSON 1

Each lesson is designed for a one-hour group session. Lessons 2-8 require preparatory work from the participant before the group session. Lesson 1, however, requires no preparation on the part of the participant.

The following schedule is how we suggest that you use the first hour of your group study:

INTRODUCTION TO THE STUDY GUIDE (10 MINUTES)

Introduce this study guide and the *God Is the Gospel* DVD. Share with the group why you chose to lead the group study using these resources. Inform your group of the commitment that this study will require and motivate them to work hard. Pray for the eight-week study, asking God for the grace you will need. Then distribute one study guide to each participant. You may read the introduction aloud, if you want, or you may immediately turn the group to Lesson 1 (starting on page 11 of this study guide).

PERSONAL INTRODUCTIONS (15 MINUTES)
Since group discussion will be an integral part of this guided study, it is crucial that each participant feels welcome and safe. The goal of each lesson is for every participant to contribute to the discussion in some way. Therefore, during these fifteen minutes, have the participants introduce themselves. You may choose to use the questions listed in the section entitled "About Yourself," or you may ask questions of your own choosing.

DISCUSSION (25 MINUTES)
Transition from the time of introductions to the discussion questions, listed under the heading "A Preview of *God Is the Gospel*." Invite everyone in the class to respond to these questions, but don't let the discussion become too involved. These questions are designed to spark interest and generate questions. The aim is not to come to definitive answers yet.

REVIEW AND CLOSING (10 MINUTES)
End the group session by reviewing Lesson 1 with the group participants and informing them of the preparation that they must do before the group meets again. Encourage them to be faithful in preparing for the next lesson. Answer any questions that the group may have and then close in prayer.

BEFORE LESSONS 2-8

As the group leader, you should do all the preparation for each lesson that is required of the group participants—that is, the ten study questions. Furthermore, it is highly recommended that you complete the entire "Further Up and Further In" section. This is not required of the group participants, but it will enrich your preparation and will help you guide and shape the conversation more effectively.

The group leader should also preview the session of *God Is the Gospel* that will be covered in the next lesson. So, for example, if the group participants are doing the preparatory work for Lesson 3, you should preview *God Is the Gospel*, Session 2, before the group meets and views it. Previewing each session will better equip you to understand the material and answer questions. If you want to pause the DVD in the midst of the session in order to clarify or discuss, previewing the session will allow you to plan where you want to take your pauses.

Finally, you may want to supplement or modify the discussion questions or the application assignment. Please remember that *this study guide is a resource*; any additions or changes you make that better match the study to your particular group are encouraged. As the group leader, your own discernment, creativity, and guidance are invaluable, and you should adapt the material as you see fit.

Plan for about two hours of your own preparation before each lesson!

DURING LESSONS 2-7

Again, let us stress that during Lessons 2-7 you may use the group time in whatever way you desire. The following schedule, however, is what we suggest:

DISCUSSION (10 MINUTES)

Begin your time with prayer. The tone you set in your prayer will likely be impressed upon the group participants: if your prayer is serious and heartfelt, the group participants will be serious about prayer; if your prayer is hasty, sloppy, or a token gesture, the group participants will share this same attitude toward prayer. So model the kind of praying that you desire your students to imitate. Remember, the blood of Jesus has bought your access to the throne of grace.

After praying, review the preparatory work that the participants completed. How did they answer the questions? Which questions did they find to be the most interesting or the most confusing? What observations or insights can they share with the group? If you would like to review some tips for leading productive discussion, please turn to the appendix at the end of this book.

The group participants will be provided an opportunity to apply what they've learned in Lessons 2-7. As the group leader, you can choose whether it would be appropriate for the group to discuss these assignments during this ten-minute time-slot.

DVD VIEWING (30 MINUTES)[1]

Play the session of *God Is the Gospel* that corresponds to the lesson you're studying. You may choose to pause the DVD at crucial points to check for understanding and provide clarification. Or you may choose to watch the DVD without interruption.

DISCUSSION AND CLOSING (20 MINUTES)

Foster discussion on what was taught during John Piper's session. You may do this by first reviewing the DVD notes (under the heading "While You Watch the DVD, Take Notes") and then proceeding to the discussion questions, listed under the heading "After You Watch the DVD, Discuss What You've Learned." These discussion questions are meant to be springboards that launch the group into further and deeper discussion. Don't feel constrained to cover these questions if the group discussion begins to move in other helpful directions.

Close the time by briefly reviewing the application section and the homework that is expected for the next lesson. Pray and dismiss.

BEFORE LESSON 8

It is important that you encourage the group participants to complete the preparatory work for Lesson 8. This assignment invites the participants to reflect on what they've learned and what remaining questions they still have. As the group leader, this would be a helpful assignment for you to complete as well. In addition, you may want to write down the key concepts of this DVD series that you want the group participants to walk away with.

DURING LESSON 8

The group participants are expected to complete a reflection exercise as part of their preparation for Lesson 8. The bulk of the group time during this last lesson should be focused on reviewing and synthesizing what was learned. Encourage all participants to share some of their recorded thoughts. Attempt to answer any remaining questions that they might have.

To close this last lesson, you might want to spend extended time in prayer. If appropriate, take prayer requests relating to what the participants have learned in these eight weeks, and bring these requests to God.

It would be completely appropriate for you, the group leader, to give a final charge or word of exhortation to end this group study. Speak from your heart and out of the overflow of joy that you have in God.

Please receive our blessing for all of you group leaders who choose to use this study guide:

> *The* LORD *bless you and keep you; the* LORD *make his face to shine upon you and be gracious to you; the* LORD *lift up his countenance upon you and give you peace. (Numbers 6:24-26)*

NOTES

1. Thirty minutes is only an approximation. Some of the sessions are shorter; some are longer. You may need to budget your group time differently, depending upon which session you are viewing.

APPENDIX
LEADING PRODUCTIVE DISCUSSIONS

Note: This material has been adapted from curricula produced by The Bethlehem Institute (TBI), a ministry of Bethlehem Baptist Church. It is used by permission.

IT IS OUR CONVICTION THAT the best group leaders foster an environment in their group that engages the participants. Most people learn by solving problems or by working through things that provoke curiosity or concern. Therefore, we discourage you from ever "lecturing" for the entire lesson. Although group leaders will constantly shape conversation, clarifying and correcting as needed, they will probably not talk for the majority of the lesson. This study guide is meant to facilitate an investigation into biblical truth—an investigation that is shared by the group leader and the participants. Therefore, we encourage you to adopt the posture of a "fellow-learner" who invites participation from everyone in the group.

It might surprise you how eager people can be to share what they have learned in preparing for each lesson. Therefore, you should invite participation by asking your group participants to share their discoveries. Here are some of our tips on facilitating discussion that is engaging and helpful:

> ❯ Don't be uncomfortable with silence initially. Once the first participant shares his or her response, others will be likely to join in. But if you cut the silence short by prompting them, they are more likely to wait for you to prompt them every time.

> Affirm every answer, if possible, and draw out the participants by asking for clarification. Your aim is to make them feel comfortable sharing their ideas and learning; so be extremely hesitant to shut down a group member's contribution or trump it with your own. This does not mean, however, that you shouldn't correct false ideas—just do it in a spirit of gentleness and love.

> Don't allow a single person, or group of persons, to dominate the discussion. Involve everyone, if possible, and intentionally invite participation from those who are more reserved or hesitant.

> Labor to show the significance of their study. Emphasize the things that the participants could not have learned without doing the homework.

> Avoid talking too much. The group leader should not monopolize the discussion but rather guide and shape it. If the group leader does the majority of the talking, the participants will be less likely to interact and engage, and therefore they will not learn as much. Avoid constantly adding the "definitive last word."

> The group leader should feel the freedom to linger on a topic or question if the group demonstrates interest. The group leader should also pursue digressions that are helpful and relevant. There is a balance to this, however: the group leader *should* attempt to cover the material. So avoid the extreme of constantly wandering off topic, but also avoid the extreme of limiting the conversation in a way that squelches curiosity or learning.

> The group leader's passion, or lack of it, is infectious. Therefore, if you demonstrate little enthusiasm for the material, it is almost inevitable that your participants will likewise be bored. But if you have a genuine excitement for what you are studying, and if you truly think Bible study is worthwhile, then your group will be impacted

positively. Therefore, it is our recommendation that before you come to the group, you spend enough time working through the homework and praying so you can overflow with genuine enthusiasm for the Bible and for God in your group. This point cannot be stressed enough. Delight yourself in God and in his Word!

desiringGod

If you would like to further explore the vision of God and life presented in this book, we at Desiring God would love to serve you. We have hundreds of resources to help you grow in your passion for Jesus Christ and help you spread that passion to others. At our website, desiringGod.org, you'll find almost everything John Piper has written and preached, including more than thirty books. We've made over twenty-five years of his sermons available free online for you to read, listen to, download, and in some cases watch.

In addition, you can access hundreds of articles, listen to our daily internet radio program, find out where John Piper is speaking, learn about our conferences, discover our God-centered children's curricula, and browse our online store. John Piper receives no royalties from the books he writes and no compensation from Desiring God. The funds are all reinvested into our gospel-spreading efforts. DG also has a whatever-you-can-afford policy, designed for individuals with limited discretionary funds. If you'd like more information about this policy, please contact us at the address or phone number below. We exist to help you treasure Jesus Christ and his gospel above all things because he is most glorified in you when you are most satisfied in him. Let us know how we can serve you!

Desiring God
Post Office Box 2901
Minneapolis, Minnesota 55402

888.346.4700
mail@desiringGod.org
www.desiringGod.org

Personal Notes

Personal Notes

Personal Notes

Personal Notes

Personal Notes

Personal Notes

Personal Notes

Personal Notes

Personal Notes

Personal Notes

Personal Notes